IT'S NOT BRAGGING IF IT'S TRUE

T0014991

IT'S NOT BRAGGING IF IT'S TRUE

ZAILA AVANT-GARDE

with MARTI DUMAS

A YEARLING BOOK

Text copyright © 2023 by Zaila Avant-garde
Cover photograph by Theodore Samuels
Hand-lettering and interior art copyright © 2023 by Charity Ekpo
Interview with Zaila copyright © 2024 by Penguin Random House LLC

Photos courtesy of the author

Visit us on the Web! rhcbooks.com

Educators and librarians, for a variety of teaching tools, visit us at RHTeachersLibrarians.com

Library of Congress Cataloging-in-Publication Data is available upon request.
ISBN 978-0-593-56899-6 (trade)—ISBN 978-0-593-56900-9 (lib. bdg.)—
ISBN 978-0-593-56901-6 (ebook)—ISBN 978-0-593-70693-0 (pbk.)

Printed in the United States of America
10 9 8 7 6 5 4 3 2 1
First Yearling Edition 2024

I dedicate this book to my parents,

for supporting *almost* every dream I have ever had.

(PE teacher never did get much support.)

CONTENTS

INTRO

have a confession to make. The title of this book is drama. I'm not lying about anything in here! But I am also not implying that anything I have done— anything worth bragging about in my life—was easy.

You're probably reading this book because you heard I am good at spelling and even better at basketball, and you're wondering how I got so good. When I say that I'm good, I'm not bragging, boasting, or showing off—it's just true. And another thing that's true is that nothing I've done to get good at spelling or basketball has been easy. Sometimes it's been lucky. Lots of times it's been fun. Sometimes it's been so unbelievably, mind-blowingly annoying that all I can do is laugh. But none of it has been easy.

In my experience, getting really, really good at something is never easy. But who says being easy is what makes something worth doing? Or even what makes it fun?

So, if you're game, I want to share the nine things that help me level up in spelling and in basketball and in everything I do. I may have done some cool stuff already, but I'm not over nine thousand yet. I still have lots of leveling up left to do and I'm still figuring out what makes me *me,* and what it will take to be the truest, ultimate version of me. If you keep reading and you follow these nine things, then we can work together, and along the way, you'll discover what leveling up—and being awesome—looks like for you, too.

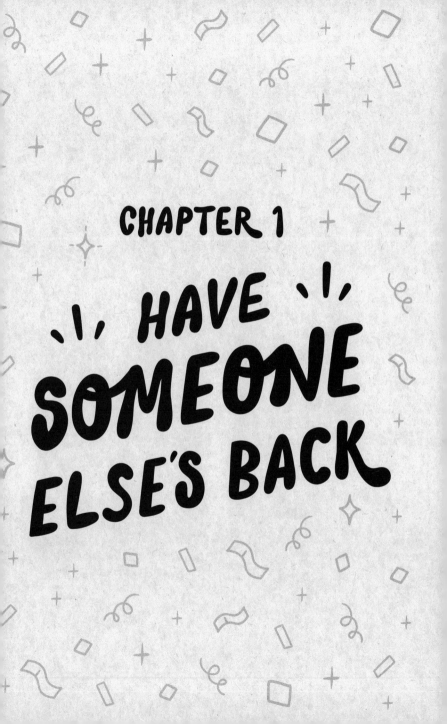

CHAPTER 1

HAVE SOMEONE ELSE'S BACK

I am homeschooled. I don't have a bell schedule. There's no cafeteria for me to eat in. No hanging out in the hallway. No lockers. None of that stuff. I can pretty much organize my day the way I want, and believe me, that is awesome. But one thing you might not realize about being homeschooled is that even though I'm not sitting in a classroom with twenty-nine other kids every day, being home-schooled means that I'm almost NEVER alone.

I have my own room and everything, but my dad or my mom or one of my brothers—or ALL of my brothers (insert eye roll here)—are somewhere close by pretty much all the time. Things can feel crowded, but crowded isn't a problem for me. I love my family. I love knowing they're nearby whenever I'm working on something. Don't get me wrong. It's not that I'm sitting there thinking, *Gee! It sure is great to have my family within two hundred feet while I practice dribbling!* It's more like a feeling that happens quietly in the background. It might sound cheesy, but it's like being surrounded by love. And also chaos. There's plenty of chaos. Except the chaos is all mixed up in the love. And it's the number one reason that if you want to level up, I think you can't start with yourself. You have to start with having someone else's back.

Having someone else's back probably seems like a weird place to begin when you want to level *yourself* up, but I have something to say that you need to hear.

Ready? Here goes.

I, Zaila Avant-garde, two-time Guinness World Record holder, winner of the Scripps National Spelling Bee, and (possible) future geneticist, am not alone. If I were alone, I would not be a two-time

Guinness World Record holder, winner of the Scripps National Spelling Bee, or anything else, because being on a team is part of what makes me a champion.

I can almost hear you saying: "But, Zaila, what about looking out for number one?"

I'm not saying you should never take care of yourself. It's just that a lot of people think that being a champion is *only* about taking care of yourself and doing what you want to do. I'm here to tell you that if you only look out for yourself, you'll never be great.

Let me rephrase that: I'm sure lots of people get great at things by hurting people, stepping on people, and thinking only about themselves. Pause and ask yourself: "Do I really want to be that person? Is that what will make me happy in the end?"

For me, the answer to both of those questions is 100 percent no!

Do you know that saying "There's strength in numbers"? In my world, having other people to look out for is a strength. It means you're a part of a group. If you're looking out for the people in your group and they're looking out for you, you don't have to be strong enough to stand on your own, because other people will have your back when you need it. Just like you'll have theirs.

Try this on for size.

I'm a big sister, and in my family, that means I'm kind of a half parent to my younger brothers. I'm not in charge of my brothers all the time, but when my father is sleeping and my mother is at work, it's my job to watch over them. With my youngest brother in the mix, believe me, that is NOT AN EASY JOB. My youngest brother is . . . well . . . I'll save that story for later. For now, let's just say that he's energetic and curious. Extremely energetic and curious. And even when my youngest brother isn't getting into things, being a big sister is a lot of work. Looking out for my younger siblings, making sure they're doing what they need to be doing, and helping them out when they need it can be a bit of a challenge, even when my parents are there.

"Zaila, what's this?"

"Zaila, open that!"

"Zaila, what does this mean?"

Being a big sister can be exhausting. In some ways, it might be easier to say, "Mom? Dad? I think you should hire a babysitter. I want to be great, so I need to spend all my time focusing on me."

Except I would never do that. Being an older sister is a really big, important part of my life, and don't tell my brothers but . . . I wouldn't trade it for anything. Yes, I'm helping them, but every time I help them, it feels good for me. It reminds me that I'm powerful enough to help someone else. Maybe not superhero-level powerful, but somewhere on the superhero spectrum.

One of my brothers is *really* into science. He's the kind of kid who always checks out books about dinosaurs and space and weather patterns from the library. And he does not try to keep whatever he is reading to himself. He talks about things like climate change a lot. Sometimes he's annoying about it. Don't get me wrong. I love science, too, and I also like to talk about it. The thing is that nine times out of ten, my brother isn't trying to talk to me—he is trying to quiz me.

"Zaila, do you know the speed of light?"

"Zaila, how far away is the sun?"

"Zaila, can you name all the types of clouds?"

If I take too long saying the answer or, heaven forbid, I don't know the answer, my brother hits me with his shocked and disappointed voice.

"Whaaaat? Why don't you know that?"

I know he's just quizzing me because he loves science so much and, since I'm the big sister, he thinks I should already know everything he does. I could definitely do without him constantly quizzing me, but the big sister in me loves to encourage him, especially about science.

That brings me to a very science-y opportunity I had. I was invited to Washington, DC, for a big event. The Smithsonian was opening a new exhibition about the future. It was really cool, and so was the fact that I'd been invited to be a speaker. At the event, it turned out that I was paired with Bill Nye. *Bill Nye!* As in Bill Nye the Science Guy. He was exactly how you would imagine him: super sweet and wearing the bow tie and everything. It was a glorious experience for me, and part of what made it so good was:

1. knowing how big a fan of Bill Nye my brother is, and
2. plotting ways for my brother to feel the glory, too.

I couldn't get a time machine to go back and bring my brother with us or develop transporter technology to whiz him there on the spot. The best thing I could do was ask Bill Nye if we could record a video of him saying hello to my brother. Believe me, the last thing I wanted was to look all dorky fangirl in front of Bill Nye. Still, I'd do it a thousand times over just to see the look on my brother's face. He was SO excited. Super excited. Uber excited. Just imagine him running around squealing, "Oh my God! This is Bill Nye!" for twenty minutes straight and you'll get the picture.

And do you know what? It felt good. Being able

to do something that would bring my brother that level of happiness is basically the definition of win-win for me. My brother was happy—win—and I was reminded that I can make a difference in someone else's life—win. Those might seem like small wins, but they aren't. It will be almost impossible to become the ultimate version of yourself if you don't believe in your power to make a positive difference in the world (even if it's just with your little brother!). The hard work I had done was paying off, and it was not just for me. It was for my whole family, which made everything I had done that much sweeter. So sweet that three hours later, when my brother came to me like he does sometimes and said, "You know, meeting Bill Nye on video was great, but I really wanted to meet him in person," all I could do was laugh and say, "Okay. Why?"

"I wanted to discuss climate change with him," he said.

Cue huge big-sister grin. "Maybe I'll meet him again. If I do, I'll bring you, and you can talk to him about climate change. In fact, I could just walk off and come back three hours later when y'all are done."

Will I get to meet Bill Nye again? Who knows. But I promise you that, on the adorable factor alone, the world deserves to hear that conversation between Bill Nye and my brother—even if it's three hours long. ☺

Now, I don't want you to get the wrong idea. Getting good stuff from having someone else's back isn't the same as making a trade. It's not like swapping chips at lunch with a friend. Yes, in that scenario maybe you wanted chili cheese and your friend wanted plain, so when you trade, you're both getting something you want instantly. That's good, but it's not what I'm talking about. On the road to leveling up, having someone else's back is less of a straight line and more of a Celtic knot. Or any kind of knot.

When I'm helping my brothers, I'm not expecting them to turn around and help me right back. I mean, they're younger than me, so they don't have as many chances to help me as I have to help them. The same thing is true when I do something for my parents. When I'm helping my mom and dad, I'm not expecting them to help me right back, either. If you do it enough, uplifting the people you love becomes a part of what you do and who you are. In a way, you're filling your space with goodness and support. And when you're surrounded with people who love you, too, that goodness and support will be there for you when you need it most.

Take my mom, for example. She's always keeping me grounded. I don't mean taking away my allowance or my privileges. I mean reminding me that parts of me are extraordinary and parts of me are ordinary, but all the parts of me are worthy of being loved. Deep, but true. That's my mom! She says no to buying me Starbucks way more than she says yes, and she hardly ever takes chores off my list, but she also drops everything to bring me to photo shoots, games, and events in California or New York or Washington, DC, without batting an eye.

And even so . . . if my little brothers are running around wild, my mom still expects me to look out for them, even if that means stopping them from throwing rocks in a parking lot right after I won the Scripps National Spelling Bee. For her, it's all the same. I'm me and I'll always be me, and as weird as that sounds, her keeping me grounded actually makes it easier for me to grow. She has my back and I have hers, too. It's not ever an even trade, but that doesn't matter. In my family, the knotty, curvy spiral of love and support surrounds us all.

Maybe you're reading that and thinking that you already can't do the very first thing because, for whatever reason, your family doesn't look or feel or behave like mine. That's okay. Just pause right here and imagine you're looking me in the eye while I say, "You are not alone."

You're not. Whoever you are, you're a part of a community, even if you have to go out and find it. You have people out there; it's just that maybe you haven't met them yet. You might have to spend a little while finding them, but once you do—whether it's a softball team or people who end up standing at the bus stop with you—you are a part of a team. And helping your team, your family, your community, reminds you that you have the power to help other people, and there are other people out there who will help you, too. There's safety in that. A messy, chaotic, beautiful safety. And feeling safe is exactly what you need to help set yourself free. That's where the real fun begins.

CHAPTER 2

WEIRD AND AROUND

You know that thing about you that you think everyone else would think was weird? Yeah. THAT thing. Cool. Well, the thing that makes you weird is probably what makes you YOU, and you should embrace it. Embrace the weird!

I'm not encouraging you to run around doing every little thing that pops into your head—especially if it's illegal—but a lot of people spend a whole lot of energy trying to be "normal," and seriously, what is normal? I know I'm not, and I wouldn't want to be!

For example, when I was a little kid, I used to go around memorizing license plates. Trust me, that is not "normal." My parents thought it was so strange that they didn't even believe me at first. One day I was riding in the car with my family. I was reading the license plates going by us, and suddenly I saw a license plate that looked familiar. I was like, "Hey, I know who's in that car."

"You recognize the car?" my father asked.

"No, I remember the license plate. It's my teammate's dad."

"Are you sure?" my parents said. And they said it in a way that made it sound like it was okay for me to be wrong. Like, I could change my mind and they wouldn't be upset or disappointed. I didn't change my mind.

"Really," I said. "I remember him saying the number that's on that license plate."

My parents just kind of looked at me. There was nothing special about the car, and neither of them recognized it. When we drove a little faster so we could see who was inside, I was right.

My parents were still skeptical. They thought maybe I had just seen the person in the car. But—and this is important—I didn't know that reading and re-membering license plates was weird. Maybe if I had, I would have doubted myself. Maybe if I had been thinking about being normal, I would have tried to come up with a more reasonable explanation to give my parents, like I had seen that father leaning on the car and remembered the way it looked. I didn't know it was strange to overhear someone talking about their license plate and still recall the number months later. So instead of shrinking back, I insisted.

The whole license plate incident sparked some-thing. If they weren't before, my parents were offi-cially on notice that I wasn't "normal," and that was a good thing. I wasn't entirely ordinary, which meant I just might be extraordinary. My father says it was a major catalyst for him. He already believed I was smart (he's the one in charge of our homeschooling), but he said that knowing I had a great memory and a strong mind encouraged him to encourage *me* to strengthen it even more. So instead of saying some-thing that might have made me feel strange or small, my father encouraged that odd little thing about me so that it would grow big.

I didn't realize at the time that owning my license plate skill was embracing the weird. It wasn't on purpose. I was just being myself. Which is exactly my point—I was being *myself,* not trying to fit into some normal-shaped box. Back then I didn't know any better, but now I do it on purpose. I am myself everywhere I go. That means I'm free to wonder about whatever I want. Ask questions about whatever I want and just let my mind go wherever my curiosity takes me. Even in the grocery store, I'm all: "Why does this apple have this name?" Or "I wonder what this tastes like?" Or "Why is this being imported all the way from Peru?" I'm sure I annoy my parents a great deal, but letting myself be free to think and wonder about all the stuff that catches my attention without worrying about looking weird has helped me out a lot.

Mental math is another great example. Mental math may not be your thing, but I love it. I don't talk much about it because I don't want to overwhelm people with all the different things I do. Right now, at the time of writing this book, I have worked my way up to multiplying and dividing six-digit numbers by five-digit numbers in my head.

I feel like I can hear your question. Are you saying, "Zaila, in a world filled with calculators, why are you multiplying big numbers in your head?" Well, I have the answer right here: because I like it! No magic. No mojo. No nothing. It's as simple as that. And it turns out, even though I didn't know it when I started, my weird little habit helped pave the way for big things. You know how I said my father encouraged me to exercise my brain in order to have a strong mind? Well, messing around with numbers in my head has helped me do that. I never would have done it if I had been worrying about being "normal." I liked it, so I did it. And when I started getting interested in spelling (more on that later!), I wasn't afraid to try it. I had already been exercising my mind with reading and curiosity and numbers, so I had no doubt I was strong enough to handle it.

What this also means is that when there are

things about myself I want to change, I am not afraid to do that, either. Embracing the weird doesn't mean never wanting to change. It might feel like the person you are today is the same person you were yesterday, but it isn't true. Billions of your cells are replaced every single day. Every twenty-four hours, about 1 percent of you is brand-new. So we're constantly changing, which makes for a great opportunity. If we're constantly changing anyway, why not work to make sure you're changing in a way that you like? At least, that's how I think of it.

Did you know that I used to be incredibly shy? Well, I still am, really. Except, unlike multiplying big numbers in my head, being incredibly shy was not a thing about myself I loved. If you're shy and you love it, good for you! In my case, being shy was holding me back because, in addition to being shy, I'm also an extrovert. That means that on most days, I love meeting and talking to new people. Being shy was seriously getting in the way of that. One time, when I was eight years old, my father took me to a basketball game. I was already really into basketball by that point, so he took me to meet one of the coaches and his player after the game. It was an amazing opportunity, but I wasn't expecting it. There were a thousand questions I wanted to ask, but I couldn't ask any of them. On the outside, I was frozen. On the inside, I was like, "Oh my God! Oh my God! Oh my God!"—freaking out and worried to the point of tears. I did not feel like myself. I felt embarrassed.

At that moment, being shy was stopping me from doing something that my heart wanted to do. Being shy is a part of me, but it was also keeping me from another important part of me: my curiosity! It almost felt like I was trapped. So, after that experience, I was like, "Zaila, this has got to change," and I decided to set myself free.

How? It was simple, but not easy. The shyness is still there inside me, after all. The difference is that now I use a ploy that lets my shyness exist without letting it take control. I imagine that every new person I meet is my grandmother. Yep. You read that right. My grandmother. If I'm meeting you for the first time, I may look relaxed and bubbly on the outside. On the inside I am struggling. While I walk over, I'm literally saying to myself in my head, "This is your grandmother, okay? It's just your grandmother," with every step. I'm really friendly with my grandmother, so for me, that works. It relaxes me just enough to let me get the conversation started, and after that, my curiosity is set free, and from there I can just be the real me.

Everybody is different, so you being the real you is definitely going to look different from me being the real me. You don't have to love math. I mean, it's cool if you do, but you don't have to. You don't have to like spelling or get weirdly curious about the fruit in grocery stores. You don't even have to like talking to other people. One thing I bet we do have in common is that when we feel free, we are filled with curiosity.

Curiosity is not just for supergeniuses. (Aside: I am not claiming to be a supergenius. [Smaller, second aside: I am also not claiming I am NOT a supergenius.]) Curiosity is just a part of being human. So, if you're human and not feeling like someone is going to judge you, your curiosity is probably popping up left and right, trying to lead you in all different directions. Let it! Let your mind wander. If something catches your attention—even just a little bit—let yourself be curious about it, no matter what other people think. And once you feel free, you usually won't even care. Well, maybe you'll still care a little bit, but it won't be enough to stop you. That's the goal. We'll call it Guilt-Free Curiosity. Has a nice ring to it, right?

So, just think about it for a minute. If Guilt-Free Curiosity reigned supreme . . . if you seriously weren't worried about being "normal," what would you let yourself do?

Roller-skate? Cool.

Draw manga? Dynamite.

Watch snails crawl across the driveway for hours at a time? Do it.

Find out how they make the fight scenes in movies look so real? Dive in!

Once you've turned yourself loose and let yourself be curious guilt-free, you'll find out you're curious about all kinds of things, even if you never thought of yourself as curious at all. Sometimes your curiosity will be tiny and only last a few seconds (or as long as it takes you to Google it), but every once in a while, you'll come across something you can't shake. You do it or watch it or read about it, and your curiosity about it just keeps growing bigger. That's when you know you've found something you're truly passionate about and it's time to dig deep and do you.

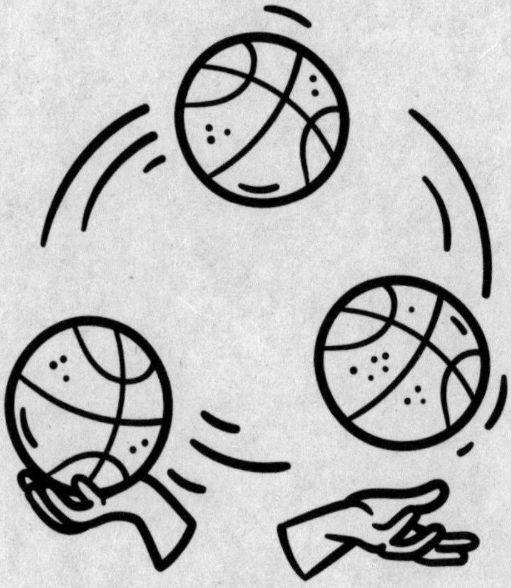

CHAPTER 3

DIG DEEP.
DO YOU.

"**O**kay, Zaila, at this point I've totally set myself free and my curiosity is popping out left and right. Now what?"

Oh! I'm happy you asked. For me, once my curiosity is flowing guilt-free, I spend a lot of time exploring the things I let myself be curious about. Since it involves a certain amount of digging, let's call it digging deep. Digging deep can help with a lot of things. Finding lost socks. Catching red ants. (Warning: I do not recommend this.) Prying open a bottle of glue. In my opinion, digging deep—and then doing you—is especially important when you're trying to become the truest version of yourself.

DIG DEEP

~~~~~~

Digging deep is exactly what it sounds like. It's also a metaphor. So unless you're digging deep about archaeology or finding clams on the beach, there are no shovels involved. This kind of digging deep is throwing yourself into something you want to learn more about. It also happens to be where I, personally, get serious. The fun kind of serious.

For things like mental math, digging deep means practicing over and over again until I know a fact as well as I know my name. For example, 7×13 is 91. Even if you meet me in person, I can say that fact really fast. It's easy because I've done it so many times and made my brain practice remembering. Practicing remembering might sound weird. A lot of people think of remembering as something you just do, not something you have to practice doing. But like with anything else, practicing makes you get stronger and stronger. In this case, I'm literally strengthening my mind, making it easier and easier for me to remember all kinds of things.

As soon as multiplying two-digit numbers by one-digit numbers got easy, I dug deeper and tried combinations that were more challenging—and I just never stopped. Why would I? Not only is doing mental math fun, but it's kind of a two-for-one. I'm digging deeper on math facts *and* digging deeper on strengthening my memory. And trust me, while having a great memory isn't everything, it's definitely a plus.

Digging deep isn't only about practice and strength. It can also be about one of my favorite things: research. I love music, but research is my *jam*. Finding out as much as I can about whatever I'm interested in makes my heart sing. It could be a big thing, like genetics, or something small-time, like coffee.

So, take coffee. I love Starbucks coffee (not sponsored). My mom likes it, too, but I could never do it the way she does it. Every time we go to Starbucks, my mom orders the same exact thing: iced chai tea latte. That's because she is not trying to be an official Starbucks aficionada. I am.

I always research my coffee. My mom never does. I already know I love Starbucks coffee, so to me that is the perfect opportunity to dig deep and explore— and it all starts with research. I pore over the Starbucks menu online, looking for new flavors, getting curious about combinations I haven't tried. My mom can keep her iced chai tea latte. Thanks to my research, every time I get coffee, it's a delicious adventure.

Coffee isn't the only thing I dig deep about. I dig deep about a lot of things. Anything I choose to go deeper on is a way of honoring who I am and what I love. Basically, it's anything that sparks my curiosity. Stuff like "Do cats have conversations?" and "Are Fuji apples actually from Japan?" gets some digging. Basketball is something I love digging into. Sometimes I dig in through books, but a lot of times I dig in by talking to coaches and other people who are good at basketball and watching them in action so I can try to copy what they're doing. I was a hyper little kid, and my parents started me with basketball when I was five so I'd have somewhere to put all my extra energy. Well, playing basketball involves learning how to dribble. Yes, I went deep on the dribbling. I went so deep doing it and watching other people doing it for hours a day that it spawned a totally new love: juggling.

I got so into juggling that, until I started spelling, the only thing I wanted for my birthday was juggling balls. Right now, I hold two world records in juggling, and there are videos of me all over the internet doing My Thing. I'm not going to sit here and tell you it was easy, but I will ask you a question: Why would being easy make it fun? I mean, tying your shoes is easy. Is it fun? Most of the time breathing is easy, too, but I never hear anybody say it's fun. The fun stuff usually involves at least a little bit of a challenge, even if that challenge is trying to imagine whether chestnut and white chocolate will make a good combo in your Starbucks order. In the case of juggling, the fun part has always been letting myself get curious about it.

Sure, I can bounce two basketballs now. Could I do three?

I can juggle four basketballs now. What happens if I throw in a ball that's a different size?

How about if I stand on a ball?

Ride a unicycle?

I've always let myself get curious about whether I can do more, and in the safety of my room with my family close by, I've always felt free to try. If I'm being completely honest, I mess up *a lot.* I guess you could say I drop a lot of balls. LOL. That doesn't stop me from being curious. I keep trying again, digging in until I can do it.

That's true of basketball skills and drills, but it's also true of all the things I'm interested in, including spelling.

At first, I thought this book would be at least half about spelling. Some people knew who I was before I won the Scripps National Spelling Bee in 2021, but the number of people who recognized me after that grew exponentially. I understand why. Being the first African American person to win the Scripps National Spelling Bee means that I broke a barrier for Black kids all around the country. It's a big deal.

I understand why people would remember me for that, and I'm glad they do. The way I've gotten to be a good speller is similar to the way I've gotten to be a good juggler or place such good Starbucks orders, and it's the same way that I'll get good at piano and genetics and the new things I'm interested in, too: I dig deep.

If you dig deep into something and you realize you're getting more and more hype about it—like I did with juggling—that's something you're passionate about. That's something you're going to want to stick with. That's something that might end up being a part of you. And that's when digging deep will help you be even more yourself. In other words, it'll help you do you.

DO YOU

What do you get hype about? Watching snails crawl across the driveway? No. Wait. I remember. It was making stick-figure flip-books about a dog who mixes particle physics with kung fu.

I kid. I kid. But the next part is really serious, so stay with me, because it's going to get deep. (No pun intended. . . . Okay, maybe pun intended.)

1. *You* are important.

I can kind of hear you over there saying something like "How would you know?" or "No, I'm not." If you're doing that, stop.

Anyway, as I was saying:

1. *You* are important.
2. The things you're passionate about are a part of you. So . . .
3. Exploring the things you're passionate about is a way of exploring yourself; therefore . . .
4. By the transitive property, exploring things you're passionate about is important.

Your Thing is important. So, you don't have to feel bad for spending a ton of time on it, and if anybody tries to make you feel bad about it you can look them in the eye and say, "It's important." Seriously. It's math.

What if you're kind of curious about something and you want to get more into it but you're not completely sure it's Your Thing? No worries! Being very interested in something doesn't mean it has to be a lifelong commitment. I mean, just because you like it doesn't mean you have to put a ring on it. If you even *kind of* think you *might* have found something that *could* be Your Thing, just keep digging deep for as long as you're having fun or until you're not curious about it anymore. If you're passionate about something, it won't be easy to shake. Even if you quit, you'll realize that you're still thinking about it, maybe even wishing you hadn't left it behind. If it nags you and encourages you to keep going, then go with it! This is the point where you go from being good at something to being *great* at something. Learning to be great at something is a skill you can practice, just like tying your shoes or riding your bike or knowing 11×12. The question is, what do you want to practice with?

I'm not going to lie: going from being pretty good at something to being great at something isn't usually easy. You have to be brave, which happens when you face your fears. My little brother is afraid of heights. If he isn't brave, he's going to miss out on a lot of fun things like roller coasters, airplane rides, and zip lines. I hope that one day he'll be brave enough to face his fear so he can get to the fun things on the other side of it. But I wouldn't want him to have to be brave literally all the time. Brave is a good thing. It also takes a lot of energy—kind of like running a marathon every single day. If you did that, you'd always be too exhausted to do anything else. In my book, it's also okay to save some of the energy you'd use for bravery and spend it on practicing instead. That's what I'm doing with singing.

If you're thinking, "Zaila, I didn't know you were a singer," you're not alone, because I'm *not* a singer. At least not yet. I just love, love, love music. One of my dreams is to be able to sing and play piano effortlessly one day, and believe me, I'm already digging deep. I used to do that under-the-breath singing, the kind where you're sort of singing but mostly you're trying to be quiet so no one will hear you. Well, one time my father heard me. "Sing up," he said.

That was easy for him to say. My father has a very nice voice. My voice is okay, but I don't always feel like it matches me. It's not easy to just "sing up" when it sort of feels like the voice coming out of you doesn't even belong to you. Even though I felt a little shy about it and I didn't think I was very good, I knew in my heart that I had to try.

So, I started digging deep, finding videos and other resources online to teach myself to sing and play the piano. I'm not good at either of those things yet, but I'm so passionate about them that I'm willing to do what it takes to be great. A lot of the stuff I'm looking at is for beginners. I don't stick to the beginner stuff, though. I know I want to be great, so I also spend a lot of time looking at what the pros do. Expanding your stomach. Breathing into the belly. Not lifting up your shoulders. There's a lot that goes into it, and I try to do what I'm learning every time I practice. Practice makes perfect! I'm not perfect yet, but I'm passionate enough to keep trying. Maybe someday I'll be brave enough to share it. Maybe you'll even hear me on a hit record one day. For now, my little brother is my only audience. He doesn't judge me, so I can put all my energy into getting better without fear.

Heads-up: the next step involves fighting, so it's going to take all the energy you can give it.

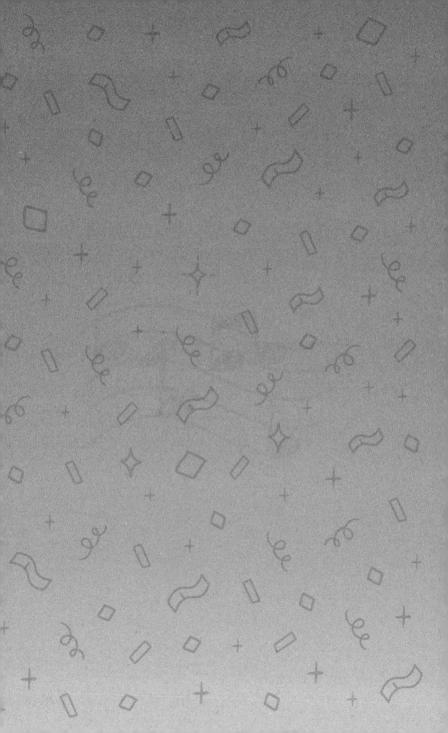

CHAPTER 4

CHOOSE YOUR OPPONENT

No, the title of this chapter is not a *Street Fighter* reference.

Well, I guess it is sort of a *Street Fighter* reference. . . . But you don't have to have played that video game to get what I'm saying. The thing is, when you're good at something, it's easy to not get better. Like, say you're good at singing. You're so good that every time you sing, people say you should go on *The Voice* or make a YouTube channel. And when people tell you that, it feels good. It's nice to get compliments, and even if you don't feel proud, you at least don't feel embarrassed. So, when it's time to sing, you sing. Choir. Karaoke. With the radio in the car. You know. Normal stuff.

Normal stuff is good. We all need good, normal stuff in our lives, so, if you like it like that, you can stop right there and enjoy singing in the car and be happy. No problem.

But . . .

(You knew there would be a "but.")

Normal may be good, but it's not *great,* and I promised to tell you how I get *great.*

If you want to be *great* at singing, you have to *choose your opponent.* Then it's Round 1: Fight!

Could you get better without having an opponent? Probably. But in my experience, it's way easier to do when I have one. It's kind of like running. I could run just for the feeling of it, and if I do that, I might even get faster. However, if I have a goal of getting as fast as possible, I don't run just for the feeling of it. I pick something to run against. Making it a race helps me put in maximum effort with all of my practice. And since it's just practice, it doesn't matter how many times it takes me to win the race.

No matter how many times you fail, you can just try again and again and again, adjusting things until, eventually, you win. You can race against a person, but you can also race against a stopwatch or your old fastest time. That's what I mean when I say you need to choose your opponent. It's kind of like setting a time that you want to beat. That doesn't only work for running. It will pretty much work for anything.

Think about spelling. For me, spelling is not me versus the other spellers. It's me versus the dictionary. Yep. You read that right. My opponent in spelling is an inanimate object. But that inanimate object is a tough opponent. I've won the Scripps National Spelling Bee, and I still have trouble beating the dictionary. At my peak, I could probably spell 98 percent of the words in the dictionary. That's a lot of words! I feel good about that. Great, even. But although 98 percent is really good, it's still not 100. That last 2 percent is what keeps me training and fighting. The more I train to fight my opponent, the better I get. Eventually, I'll win.

Spelling is cool because when I'm racing against

the dictionary, I'm actually racing two opponents—root words and my own memory.

I can almost hear you saying, "Zaila, are you really over there fighting with yourself?" Sort of? LOL.

I think of it more like challenging myself. Do you remember that story about me and the license plates? Maybe I've always had a talent for memorizing things, but that talent would have gone nowhere if I hadn't spent so much time practicing it. My father always says your brain is like a muscle. Just like The Rock works out all the time to grow huge muscles, I work out my brain, honing my memory into a sharp, powerful skill. I absolutely hate when people say things like "Oh. You're just memorizing." First of all, memorizing isn't the only thing I do, and second of all, there's no *just* with memorizing. It's a skill I've worked hard on and am really proud of.

When I work on making my memory stronger, I always want to do a little bit more than I could before. I am absolutely challenging myself, but it's not a fight. It's fun, like trying to top your own high score at *Beat Saber* or any other game. Even when you lose, you're still the winner. Competing against myself would not have been enough to become a spelling champion. When I did that, I was doing pretty well at spelling bees, but I didn't start winning the top prizes until I chose a tougher opponent: root words.

Root words make awesome opponents because they're so interesting, and the more you run after them, the more you want to know. It's not just re-membering spelling. It's not even just knowing the meanings of the words. I'm digging deep so I can actually know the story of the word. Know where it comes from and how it got there.

A common misconception about competitive spellers is that we only know how to spell words. Kids have literally said to me, "You just know how to memorize words. Good for you." Wrong. The best spellers don't just memorize words. We know what the words mean. We know where they come from. We will apply these words to our life later, because studying the roots takes us so deep that we actually get reconnected to the world. Like, for example, the

Ogooué River. The Ogooué is a river in Gabon, in Africa. You look at it, and you think, "If this river is in Africa, why is it spelled like a French word?" So you do a little bit more research, and you're like, "Oh! Colonialism. The country was colonized by the French. So they were forced to take on the French language, and that's why the name of a river in Africa is spelled like French." There's always a story like that, and they're all different. That's what makes root words tough. It's also the thing that makes me love spelling.

Picking a tough opponent is part of the path to greatness. It gives you a reason to keep challenging yourself, even when you know you're already good. And I never have and never will choose another speller as my opponent, not even at a spelling bee. In fact, at spelling bees, I'm literally rooting for everybody. Seriously. When any person goes up onstage at a spelling bee, I instantly feel their pain. Being onstage is nerve-racking. And let's say they get the word "cat" and start off with "k"? Inside, I'm like, *Nooooooooo,* and I feel terrible. I know the bell's gonna tell them they got the word wrong, and I know they're going to be really sad when it happens. I also know there's nothing I can do about it. I just sit there waiting for the moment when the bell rings and it feels awful.

So, no. No other speller is ever my opponent. In fact, I try not to even compare myself to other spellers. Maybe that's partly to be kind to them, but it's also being kind to me! People have feelings, and people can definitely get hurt. In my book, unless you want to go back to that supervillain thing in chapter one ☺, picking an actual person as your opponent is a terrible idea. That especially goes for teammates, even if you're not the one doing it.

Are you thinking: "Wow, Zaila! That was an incredibly specific transition. Do I smell a story coming?"

Yes, you do. And I'm sorry to say it's not a pretty one. Actually, it's so un-pretty that I'm not even going to use people's real names.

I had this coach. Let's call him Bob. Coach Bob. So, Coach Bob coached one of my basketball teams when I was younger. Overall, Coach Bob was a nice person and a pretty good coach. He just had one awful habit: comparing people. Specifically, he had a habit of comparing the other girls on the team to me. He'd say things like:

"Look at the way Zaila is doing it."

"Copy what Zaila is doing."

"Why can't you do it the way Zaila is doing it?"

I hated when he did that. I'd just be sitting there, minding my own business, and for no good reason Coach Bob was making me a target. Every time he did that, it set me up for disaster. The kids he was telling to be more like me always seemed to either pass the ball a little too hard or not pass it to me at all. You'd think I'd be upset with my teammates. After all, they were the ones who were being rough with me. I wasn't upset with my teammates. I was upset with our coach because he wasn't being fair. I had been practicing basketball skills almost every day since I was five, while most of my teammates had just started playing. But the worst part was that by constantly comparing me to my teammates, it didn't feel like he was making a stronger team. It felt like he was making me their enemy. He was setting me up as their opponent when I wasn't. I was their teammate. All of us should have been growing together and rooting for each other while we did. That's what makes a good team.

As frustrating as that whole experience was, I learned something. Two things, actually.

1. Choose your opponent wisely.
2. You are beyond compare. No matter where you are in your journey, it's your journey. Enjoy your joy.

And you're going to need every drop of joy you can get. So, instead of choosing another person to go after, consider choosing something like root words. It definitely worked for me. In fact, calling for definitions was something I became known for. It was flashy, like a behind-the-back pass in basketball. Are behind-the-back passes absolutely necessary? No. They're a way of showing out. In my world, *showing up* and *showing out* are right there on the road to being great.

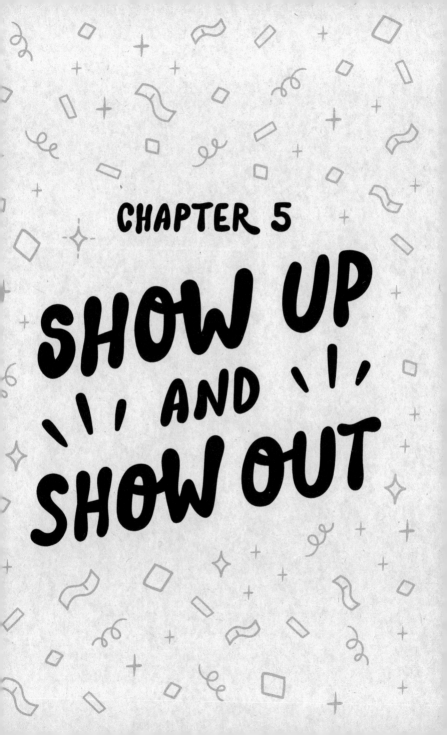

CHAPTER 5

SHOW UP
AND
SHOW OUT

Brace yourself. It's time for a little tough love.

Life is not a fairy tale.

You are not automatically destined for success from birth.

But! you can put yourself on the path to success by working hard.

I know that telling people they're not destined for success isn't exactly going to get me a million upvotes. The thing is, even though I'd love to have a million likes and ten million subscribers, the whole point of me writing this book is to maybe, possibly be helpful. I don't know how other people do it, but there is no way I'll be helpful if I don't tell you the truth. And the truth is:

Life is not a fairy tale.

You are not automatically destined for success from birth.

But! you can put yourself on the path to success by working hard.

I can almost hear you saying, "But, Zaila, you said that if I let myself be curious, found something I really wanted to do, and chose the right opponent to encourage me to grow, I'd be able to do literally anything!"

Did I say that? Okay. Fair. I can see how you might have gotten that. Allow me to clarify.

Even if you have a supportive community and you are talented and curious and you choose your opponent, the way to go from good to great is to work hard.

Are there shortcuts?

No.

Fairy godmothers?

No.

Cheat codes?

No.

There is only SHOWING UP and SHOWING OUT.

I'm not going to sit here and tell you that you can run through flash cards once a week or practice basketball five minutes a day and become great. I guess, technically, it's possible. So is winning the lottery, getting struck by lightning, and seeing a black bear, grizzly bear, and polar bear in the wild all in the same day. It probably won't happen, but sure, technically, it's possible. If you like those odds, take them. If not, keep reading.

SHOW UP

To me, showing up means you are doing something with a very strong level of effort consistently. Like, every day. And you can't do that without preparation and conditioning. Preparation is whatever you do to get ready for something, which probably includes lots of practice. Practice looks very different depending on what you're trying to get good at. If you want to do great on a math test, your practice might be doing math problems. If you're trying to become great at drawing, you might be practicing lines and shapes, or shading. But what some people count as practice, I would barely call a warm-up. If that sounds scary, that's okay. You don't have to jump into practicing something for seven hours every day just because you heard I do that. You're not competing with me, remember? The only thing you have to do is a little more than you're used to. If you want to show up for, say, multiplication facts, and yesterday you studied them for zero minutes, today try practicing them for five minutes. Then move to ten minutes. Then fifteen. Depending on what your goal is, you may never have to get close to working on it for seven hours at a time. That's not how it was for me, though, at least not when it came to spelling.

I wanted to be great at spelling, so I practiced the words that appear in the Scripps National Spelling Bee most frequently. There are lots of them, and every day I did 13,000 of them. If I only wanted to be good, I could have just leaned on the words I already knew. I knew a lot! In fact, before I ever decided to be a speller, my father kind of tested me on it. He was watching the Scripps National Spelling Bee and got curious about how I would have done, so he quizzed me about all the words in the final round. He was doing it for fun, and I got nearly every single one right. That was good. Realizing I was already kind of good at spelling made me curious to know if I could be *great*. So I practiced. When I say practice, I mean repeating something so many times that it basically becomes a part of you. Like, maybe you make a mistake, but that mistake would be one out of a hundred times, not one out of ten. So, to get there, I used a program called SpellPundit, and I practiced spelling words for seven hours a day. Over time, I worked my way up to spelling 13,000 words all in one day.

Conditioning is not just the skill you're practicing; it's how long your mind and body will let you do it well. When I first started spelling, I would get pretty tired. Over time, I gradually built up stamina. By practicing for seven hours, I was conditioning my brain to focus on spelling for almost an entire day, which, coincidentally, is exactly what you have to do when you're at a regional or national spelling bee.

Not everything takes seven hours a day to prepare. The best basketball team that I was ever on only practiced three hours a day, four days a week. I'm homeschooled, but I got to play on my local middle school team. Even though we only practiced three hours a day, we worked super hard. Everybody showed up for every practice. I don't just mean that they were present; I mean that everyone was trying their best and really working to improve. We probably practiced harder than any other middle school. Our coach worked us like we were a college team. He had us running outside, running up flights of stairs, and coming down and doing push-ups. It was intense. And that was before we ran drills. We worked so hard together that at a certain point, we could be as goofy as we wanted and not have it knock us off our game. That's when things really got fun.

Before games, we'd be on the court with the other team, doing warm-ups. On their end of the court, the other teams looked super organized, doing their lay-up lines. One person does a lay-up, another person rebounds. It's supposed to be a serious thing. My team, on the other hand, would be laughing, goofing up, and just having fun. In our lay-up lines, we'd be throwing the ball behind our back, not paying attention. The rebounding people were literally doing cartwheels. It was just a mess. A hilarious mess. If you looked at us, I'm sure you would have been like, "What is this?"

We were so silly that the other teams took one look at us and stopped taking us seriously. We were also so prepared and so well conditioned that once we hit the court, we knew everything would click into place. Sometimes the other teams would shake their heads at us or give us disapproving looks. That was usually as far as it went, but this one time we were playing our rival team and they took it further.

They were actually saying mean things about us where we could hear them. My teammates and I just shrugged. We knew that any comebacks we came up with would be nothing next to what we showed them on the court.

How did we do? Well, where I'm from in Louisiana, there's something called the mercy rule. It means that if you're beating another team by thirty points before the third quarter, you take mercy on them and let the game end right there. Let's just say that we took mercy on them. The other team looked like they had no idea what had just happened to them. Their coach was just shaking her head. The girls looked completely confused. They were so serious the whole time, but somehow they had gotten totally beaten by a group of kids who they thought were just messing around. The thing is that, while being serious can help you get prepared, just being serious doesn't automatically mean you are prepared. My team showed up in practice. We were prepared. In fact, we were so prepared that when we got to the game, we could actually show out.

SHOW OUT

Showing out is having fun while giving your all. It comes *after* you've been showing up. Showing out means that you're so prepared and so well conditioned, you can have a lot of fun. Showing out is a good thing, and I love to see other people doing it. It's really inspiring. In fact, I just recently realized that my grandfather's second wife was the first African American woman to get a PhD in astrophysics. I had no idea! I just found the article and I was like, "Hey! That's my grandfather's wife." Here was this African American woman doing excellent things, pushing for stuff in a field where she definitely wasn't accepted. Seeing her like that gave me another shoulder to stand on. It was so inspiring. If no one had ever written about her work, made her show out a little, I never would have known. Seeing her be great makes it that much easier for me to try to be great, too. That article about her wasn't bragging. It was just true.

Whatever you do, don't get showing out confused

with showing off. Showing out is not about pretending to have done a lot of hard work when you really haven't. Showing out isn't bragging or trying to make yourself look better by making someone else feel worse. Showing out is about the joy of hard work and accomplishment. It's when you've practiced so much that you can't help but shine. Whenever I'm practicing something, showing out might be one of my ultimate goals. That doesn't mean it's easy to do. In fact, there's no way I would have been able to get there about anything at all if I weren't willing to *ask for help*.

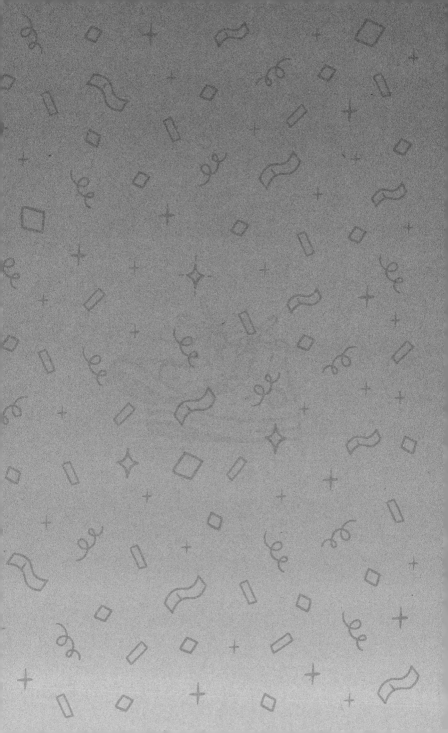

CHAPTER 6

ASK FOR HELP

(And don't turn down help when it's offered.)

I get it. You're stubborn and sometimes you would rather do things on your own.

My bad. I'm definitely talking about me on that.

We all have stuff we need to work on, and asking for help is one of those things for me. It's not exactly that I don't want help. It's more that I feel weird about asking. When I decided I wanted to participate in my first spelling bee, even though I figured my father would approve, I was still afraid to ask. I waited until my grandmother asked me what I wanted for my birthday to spring it on her. She was pretty shocked, but no one was more shocked than my father. It wasn't that my grandmother told him I wanted to compete in a spelling bee instead of the pizza, cake, and juggling balls I had asked for every year since I was five. It was that I hadn't asked him in the first place.

I think I was afraid my father might say no, so I ambushed him by having my grandmother ask instead. My grandmother is my father's mother, after all. I knew he wouldn't tell *her* no.

These days I wouldn't go through that much scheming to get help, but it took a long time for me to get there. I had to come up against my own limits again and again. It kept happening with spelling, even several stages in. After I won my regional spelling bee, I got the list of words that my first-round word in the Scripps National Spelling Bee would come from. The list was 4,000 words long, and I only had about six months to prepare. I was studying with, of course, SpellPundit and online flash cards my father made. Because of those flash cards and SpellPundit, I worked my way up to practicing 10,000 words a day. That may sound impressive, but

I was struggling. And the worst part of it wasn't the spelling; it was waiting for the internet to load.

Our internet connection was *the worst.* That's when my father jumped in to help. He couldn't make the internet go faster, so instead, he got another computer. I'd use one computer while the other was loading and switch back and forth between them. I cannot explain to you what a big deal that two-computer setup was. Because of it, I was finally able to get through 13,000 words in one day. Knowing that I consistently had the stamina and know-how to spell every single one of the most common Scripps words in one day was a serious game-changer. Once I could do that, my confidence went through the roof. And you know what? It almost didn't happen. Back then, I just let myself struggle, hitting this wall of 10,000 words a day over and over again without saying a thing. I'm pretty smart, but that wasn't a smart thing to do. Yes, it worked out in the end, but what if my father hadn't noticed? If I had it to do over again, I would tell him what was happening sooner and actually ask him to help me solve the problem.

* * *

My grandfather, my father's father, should have his own book written about him—his story is that inspiring. He worked at Sears, and then he went back and got his high school degree at twenty-seven years old. He didn't stop there, though, and went on to become a physics professor. My whole life, he's been one of those people who just picked themselves up, looked themselves in the mirror, and were like, "Let's do something." And for the longest time, I was afraid to talk to him. Remember the thing about me being shy? Well, when my grandfather was around, I'd be ducking into corners and hiding under beds, afraid to say anything. But I'm so glad that those days are behind me!

My grandfather and I don't live in the same place, but as soon as I asked him to help me with my growing interest in math and physics, he agreed. My gregarious, white-haired grandfather has taken on a much bigger role in my life, tutoring me in math and physics over Skype. Asking for his help has helped me excel at a NASA program where all of the kids are way older than me.

See? Asking for help is a good thing. I think it's best to learn and do what you can on your own first, but asking for help once it's clear you need it is a good thing. I don't have a voice teacher or a piano teacher yet, but I won't be shy about asking for them when the time comes, and I've had lots more chances to practice asking for help in the meantime.

In 2019, I thought I was as prepared as I could be for the Scripps National Spelling Bee. I wasn't. I had practiced and done everything I could on my own, and I still hadn't reached my goal. Luckily, by then I wasn't going to leave it up to chance. I knew I needed to ask for help. I was nervous about it at first. Then I thought of my goal, took a deep breath, and asked anyway. My family came through. They got me a private coach who had done very well in Scripps himself, Cole Shafer-Ray. Working with Cole was another game-changer. Like my other good coaches, Cole understood that it wasn't me against other spellers, it was me against the dictionary. Because he was already an experienced speller, he didn't just try to cover up my weak spots, he tried to make what I was good at even stronger. He knew I could memorize a lot of words and their meanings, but instead of focusing on whole words, Cole deepened my roots (you know, the roots of words).

Take "polyphagia," for example. "Poly" means many. If you learn the root "poly," you don't just know how to spell the beginning of "polyphagia"— you also know how to spell the beginning of "polyangiitis," "polyphosphate," and all the other "poly" words. Some roots are connected to thousands of words. Focusing more on roots means that instead of learning one word at a time, I was sometimes getting parts of hundreds or thousands of words at a time. Cole challenged me in a way that I might never have thought to challenge myself. His experience meant that he could dig and find roots that I had never even heard of. Roots I might never have seen if he hadn't known how to dig for them. He'd throw them at me, hoping to trip me up. Strangely, I actually liked when he could. It meant I was learning something new, which meant I was getting stronger. Getting help from Cole sent my spelling game into the stratosphere. Sure, I had to keep showing up, practicing every day so that someday I really would be ready to show out. It was hard work, and it didn't always feel great, but that's all a part of *rolling with the punches.*

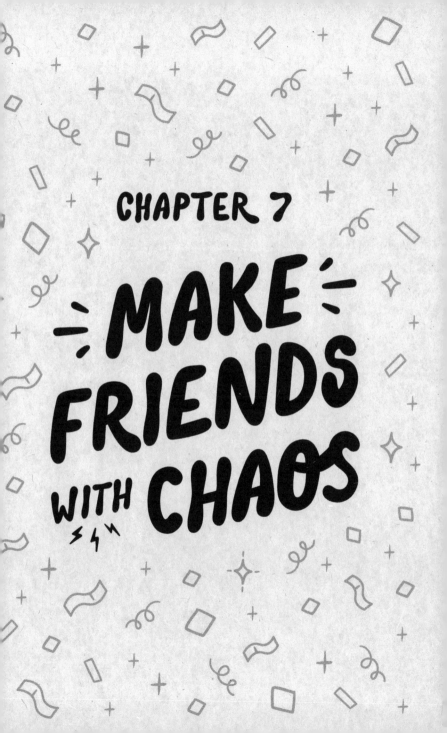

CHAPTER 7

MAKE
FRIENDS
WITH CHAOS

Some days, the world is like bowling. All the balls and pins are nicely lined up. Everyone patiently waits for their turn to try to knock the pins down. If you knock all the pins down on your turn, that's great! If not, no problem! You can just wait for your next turn.

The world isn't always like bowling, though.

Sometimes the world is dodgeball. Everyone is on the field at once. Nothing is calm or orderly. Things are literally getting thrown at you from every direction. It's chaos. Standing there, it might be easy to feel like there's nothing you can do except wait for somebody to get you out. But there is something you can do. You can duck and weave and dodge. That's rolling with the punches. It's not something I learned on purpose, but boy am I glad I did.

It all started with noisy little brothers. I told you that when my mom and dad are busy, I'm kind of a half parent to my little brothers. What I didn't finish telling you is that one of my brothers is *wild*! Like, double-underline, extra-exclamation-points wild.

I can almost hear you saying, "Seriously, Zaila? You aren't exaggerating even just a little bit? I mean, how wild can one little brother be?"

Sure, he's pretty adorable. He loves apples and likes to tuck them into weird places around the house. He runs and yells and has a ton of energy. Usually when I study, he'll be crawling all over me, banging on my keyboard. Having my youngest brother there, banging on the keyboard and making wild sounds while I was studying, meant I really had to learn to focus. I was going through the hardest words in the dictionary with a baby who was deter-mined to distract me. Even with him climbing on my shoulders and practically bouncing off my head, I still managed to make it through my 13,000 words a day. Compared to that, you can imagine how, once I was just onstage with everybody being quiet and no baby to stop from falling, spelling words was a piece of cake. I hate to say it, but I think, in a way, it was helpful. Instead of being a curse, my distracting little brother was a blessing in disguise.

Then there's mistakes during a bee. Every time I misspell a word, it's a chance for me to learn something new, something that will make me better next time. My tutor, Cole, practically made it his mission to get me out on words when we practiced. He couldn't always do it, but every time he did, I learned something. And, in a weird way, it helped me roll with the punches. I knew I was working my hardest, so when the competition came around, whatever happened was okay. I wouldn't be telling myself, "Zaila, you could have studied harder," because I couldn't have studied any harder. I was showing up every day, putting everything I had on the table, and that was the best I could do. I'm not gonna say I was always smiling after losing a bee, but eventually I began to believe that whatever happened, it was the best outcome.

There's something else you should know, and chances are, you might not want to hear it. . . .

Doing enough doesn't always mean you'll win.

Movies and shows like to tell you that if you put in maximum effort, you'll automatically get what you're going for. That you'll become a Karate Kid or a Super Saiyan or whoever is destined to win the day. Those are great stories, but I promised to tell you things honestly—and honestly, no matter how awesome you are, no matter how prepared you are, you will not always win.

And—*plot twist!*—winning every time is not the point. Seriously. It's probably not even good for you.

The ultimate you is always going to be human. Humans have good days and bad days. Humans win sometimes and lose sometimes. But when you're trying to be great at something or a lot of things, a huge part of that is learning to roll with the punches. That means learning how to lose and how to turn those losses into steps toward a win.

Think about it. Even Serena Williams doesn't win every match. If you came in first every single time you did something, it would get sad pretty quickly. Ever seen *One-Punch Man*? It's about this guy who discovers that he can basically defeat any creature in the universe with one punch. That sounds good, right? Except, it isn't. It's boring. He knows he'll win and every time he does, he's disappointed because, until he faces something that can challenge him, he'll never know how good he actually is and he'll never be able to grow. He's stuck.

One-Punch Man is fiction. You and I are very real. Every time we lose, we learn something new about ourselves. We learn how tough we really are. We learn how tough we want to be. We learn what mistakes we've made and, since we're trying to level ourselves up, we'll make a strategy that will hopefully help us grow and not make that mistake again. If that strategy works, great! We'll do it again. If it doesn't work, we'll try something different.

In a way, that's where the maximum effort comes in. You haven't lost until you've quit, so keep going. Keep putting in maximum effort. It may not guarantee that you win every time, but it does guarantee that you're on the path to being the most you *you.*

When I competed in my first online spelling bee, I had already won my regional spelling bee and participated in the 2019 Scripps National Spelling Bee. Winning the regional bee was kind of easy. Sure, I practiced, but nothing I would consider strenuous. Nothing I would consider maximum effort. Which is why I got to my first online bee and felt very confident. I'm not saying I thought I would definitely get first place, but let me tell you that I was not prepared to get one hundredth place, which is exactly what I got.

After that, I spent a while feeling bad. I can't go into too much detail because I honestly don't let myself go back to that memory very often. I was definitely disappointed and upset and it did not feel good. At the same time, even while I was upset, I was pushing myself to get past it. I was telling myself things like "You don't have a time machine. You can't go back and change it. So, leave that part of the past in the past and figure out what you're going to do in the future."

I believe in that whole idea of chipping away at things. I thought of that meme with the rock. *Keep chipping away. Keep chipping away.* It was tough, and since I love spelling so much, the fact that I didn't win was even tougher. I kept chipping away at my disappointment, though. Getting past it was my new goal. Eventually, I was able to say to myself, "You know what? It's actually a good thing I tanked that spelling bee. Now I know what I need to do. My goal is right on the other side of the wall. If I put in some more effort, my next hit might be the one that breaks through."

Spoiler alert: it worked.

I set a new goal. The goal wasn't getting first place every time. The goal was never getting below sixth. That was a goal I could hit. I hit it every time and I was happy about it, even though sixth place is nowhere near winning.

Winning every time isn't the point, remember? It's all about maximum effort toward your goal. Putting in maximum effort may not guarantee that you win, but it does guarantee that you're on the path to becoming the ultimate you. And the ultimate you will ultimately win because the ultimate you is always trying to be a little bit better than last time. You don't have to win every single time to do that. If you*:

1. actually stop and examine your losses,
2. ask for help,
3. adjust your plan, and
4. get back at it,

you'll keep chip-chip-chipping away at that wall, and before you know it, you'll break through.

*I left a part out of that list. I didn't leave it out because it isn't important. I left it out because I don't know where it goes. For me, it changes around every time, so I'll just add it here: Sulk. Pout. Brood. Wail and moan and gnash your teeth. Shout out to the heavens. Whatever you want to call it, don't worry if you need to take a little time to feel bad and lick your wounds. I do! Being human means things hurt us. You probably won't get to your goal without at least a little drama. Or trauma. Or both. Pouting may be a part of the process, but it's a temporary stop, not a place to live. I'm giving myself time to feel and rest so that I can turn those frustrations and disappointments into fuel for the next round of work. That's the biggest part of rolling with the punches! The more I do it, the easier it is to let things go and let myself get clicked into the zone.

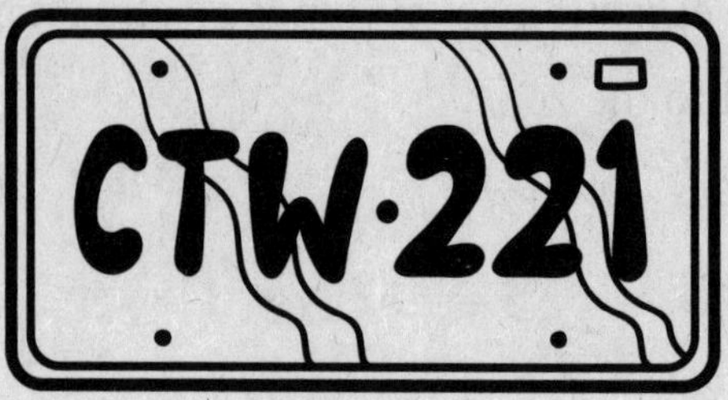
CTW·221

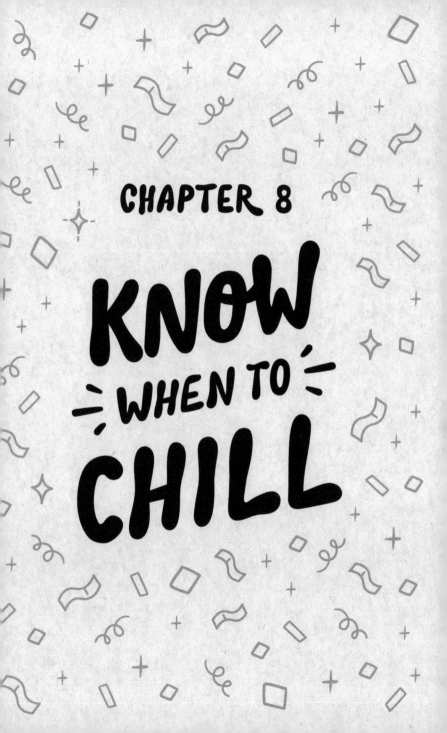

CHAPTER 8

KNOW
WHEN TO
CHILL

You know how I keep saying we're human? To be honest, it's as much a reminder for me as it is for you. Sometimes when you're working on something that's important to you and you're trying your best to get it right, you might wish you were a robot or a cyborg or someone in *The Matrix*—whatever it would take to make perfection as easy as downloading a new app or operating system.

Piano, virtuoso level: Uploaded!

Inventor, master level: Unlocked!

Geneticist, Nobel Prize level: Skill attained!

That would be *awesome.* And if we ever get there

technologically, I'll be the first one in line. (Or second in line, to confirm that the tech is actually safe!)

In the meantime, we'll have to deal with being 100 percent human. Being human means that sometimes you have to rest your mind and your body, even when you want to finish editing that video or perfecting that skill on the balance beam or getting to whatever the next step is that's closer to your goal. That's a good thing! It means you know what you want and you won't quit until you get it. But part of getting better is learning how and when to *chill*. Being tired is not the goal. If I didn't stop and spend time recharging, I would not be able to keep trying to level up.

Have you ever waited too long to charge one of your devices? Like, have you let your phone or your VR headset get down to 2 percent before you plug it in? Well, I have, and the results aren't pretty. Say I'm playing *Beat Saber* on my VR headset and I'm trying to beat my high score. When I get the battery low warning, I have two choices: plug it in, or ignore it and keep playing. And you know how it is—if I plug it in, it's annoying to play with the VR headset plugged in. The cord isn't long, so I have to hold my head a certain way and I can't move as much as I want to. If I ignore it, I can probably play a few more minutes, but then the headset charges out anyway. Once the headset charges out, it takes forever to be able to turn it back on, even when you plug it in.

People are like VR headsets. We need a chance to recharge, and it's better if we don't wait until the last minute to do it. If I keep pushing and pushing myself until I burn out, it takes me an incredibly long time to recover. That's why I think it's been so important for me to find my Zen. Which is another way of saying find my calm or my chill or my balance.

Eating dinner is a prime example of that. The whole homeschooling thing means I spend lots and lots of time with my family, so we don't usually sit down to dinner together. I kind of love it. My younger brothers tend to eat at the table, but I take my dinner and eat it when I want and where I want. Sometimes that means eating dinner while I watch a basketball game. The rhythm of it, the sound, and the movement of the game relax me. Even if nothing else has helped me feel calm and still all day, watching basketball over dinner totally will. It's like plugging myself in to recharge. That's what makes it one of the small ways I find my Zen.

It's not always basketball, though. I love watching old TV shows like *Family Matters* or *Everybody Hates Chris*. Those shows are hilarious, and who doesn't love to laugh? Watching comedy shows is one of the little ways I plug myself back in to recharge. I don't just like watching comedy—I like to watch people while *they* watch comedy. I love seeing what makes people laugh. Figuring out how to make other people laugh is like a puzzle I'm always trying to solve. It doesn't work every time, although sometimes I do pull off some good ones! It feels great to figure out what makes someone laugh or smile, because I know how good it feels when I'm laughing and smiling, too. Laughing and smiling are two of my favorite activities—they make me feel refreshed and recharged almost instantly. That's one of the reasons I still love playing and hanging out with my little brothers. Have you ever seen an adorable little kid be extra serious about something like the distance from the sun to Pluto or what exactly would happen if you tried to land on Jupiter? My brothers do things like that all the time. They're hilarious, even when they don't mean to be. I feel happier just getting to spend time with them being themselves.

Even in a house full of brothers, I still find ways to plug in and escape. I like to listen to NPR. Yep, that is National Public Radio. Nope, I am not an old person. Listening to something like *Fresh Air* is great because I can relax and listen to Terry Gross ask a smart person a bunch of questions I would want to know the answers to, and Terry Gross does all the work. I can just sit back and enjoy. (Full disclosure: sometimes listening to those interviews and articles on NPR makes me so curious about something that I launch into research mode, but I promise that it's still recharging my battery.)

Another small way I find my Zen is reading books. I love books like *Dead Man Walking* by Sister Helen Prejean. Reading "The Eyewitness Account of the

Death Penalty That Sparked a National Debate" is not exactly what you'd call chill. Important, but not chill. You know what is chill? Hobbits. The hobbits in Tolkien's fantasy books are extremely chill. They spend their lives eating and hanging out in the Shire without too many troubles at all. I think that's why I love fantasy books so much. Letting my mind float and relax and seriously think about something as unserious as an orc redemption arc helps recharge my battery.

Joking around with my family, reading, listening to NPR, and watching TV are all great, but that's the stuff I do on a regular day. Competition days are different. On competition days, I need to find my Zen in a big way, because on competition days I need to get in the zone.

Do you know what helps me find my Zen so I can get in the zone? Coffee. Sometimes my mom gets me a coffee from Starbucks (not sponsored, but, Starbucks, if you're out there, you should totally sponsor me ☺), but most of the time it's the kind you get in glass bottles at the grocery store. On days I really need to get into the zone, I start by drinking one of those. Then I put on my headphones and listen to music. I love all kinds of music, so I listen to whatever I'm in the mood for. Old-school rap. Soul. Sometimes it's Christmas music, even in July. The important thing isn't the time of year, it's that the music matches my mood. On days when I can't listen to music—if I have something happening in my day where I have to leave in the morning and I can't listen to music when I come back—I get physically sad and depressed. Not listening to music makes me feel worse. It's like I'm Elliott and music is E.T. We have a physical connection.

Listening to music is especially important on competition days because music lets my mind feel calm and free. Music and coffee make a perfect combination. When I have both of those things, my day is all Zen and focus. I don't think about anything except the competition or whatever the big thing is ahead of me. Unlike most days, when I'm thinking about my family and my community and having other people's backs, this is the time I choose to focus on myself. I put on my headphones and listen to music. I sip my coffee. I breathe. I quiet my mind. I keep my body calm and focused. I can do that because I've practiced doing it lots of times. My Zen routine helps me concentrate on the fact that I am ready. I know in my heart that I have truly prepared as much as I could. I showed up every day. If I'm calm and focused, when it's time to perform, I'll be able to show out.

Everybody in my family helps. They already know:

"Don't talk to Zaila."

"This is a spelling day."

"Zaila needs to be calm."

So, when my family helps me make space to focus just on myself and the things I want to accomplish, my Zen doesn't just stop me from burning out. It also helps me get into the zone.

The zone is a place where all my preparation and conditioning take on a life of their own. When I'm in spelling bees, I'm so focused. I'm focused and I'm in the zone and once I leave that zone, I don't quite remember being in it. It's the same as it is in sports. It's like, for a little while, the player and the game become one thing. The player doesn't need to think. The player can just play, and since they're a part of the game, it mostly plays smoothly. That's called being in the zone. That's what it's like for me. Something just clicks.

By the time competition day rolls around, it's not time for practicing or conditioning. It's time to play. It's time for the zone. If you want to get there, you have to find your Zen.

The way you find your Zen might be different from mine. Maybe you run laps or play jacks or go strip-mining in *Minecraft*. The point isn't *how* you do it. The point is *that* you do it. Because once you've found your Zen and clicked into the zone, there's only one thing left to do: *win*.

$$\Delta x = vt - 1/2 at^2$$

$$v^2 = v0^2 + 2a\Delta x$$

CHAPTER 9

WIN

have a confession to make: I almost always win.

Not because I'm supersmart.

Not because I'm superskilled.

Not because I'm supertalented.

I win because I don't quit.

I can almost hear you now: "But what I'm into is not even a competition. How can I win?"

I'm very happy you asked! Winning isn't always about being in a race or a spelling bee or a basketball game. Winning is about being successful, and the cool part about success is that *you* get to define what success is. Sure, your teachers and parents and neighbors will have ideas about what success means to them. And if they have your best interests at heart, you probably want to take their ideas into consideration. At the end of the day, you're the *only* person who can define what success means to you.

Success is doing well at something you truly like. It might involve trophies or awards, but it absolutely doesn't have to. I didn't have those kinds of accolades until I was ten—and even then it was just a little plate I got for winning a competition in my neighborhood. I still hold on to that plate and I treasure it greatly, but that plate is not success. The fact that I didn't get a trophy until I was ten does not mean I wasn't good at stuff. It doesn't mean I wasn't great at stuff. I mean, at that point I was elite at multiple things! Getting that plate wasn't suddenly proof that I was great—I was already being successful. Success does not have to be something that's recognized by other people. It's great to get trophies and go to nationals, but success can also be something no one else sees. Success is setting a goal and working until you get there. It doesn't have to be big. It doesn't have to be something you declare to the whole world. It can be something small that you hold inside yourself.

I just started piano. I've mostly been teaching myself using apps and tutorials. I might go faster if I had a teacher, but I like working through some of the early parts alone. That way, when I do get a teacher, I'll already have some of the easy stuff down. I don't need anyone to tell me to practice the C major scale. LOL. I can do that on my own. Anyway, as I progressed, I started learning the Beatles song "Hey Jude." I set tiny goals for myself. Just get a few seconds right at a time. Every time I hit one of those small goals, it felt good. It felt like a win because it was a win. The first time I played the whole song was super exciting. There was nobody around. Nobody heard me playing. Nobody heard that it happened. It was just for me. It was success just for me. No trophies. No publicity. Nothing but me in that moment of playing "Hey Jude" straight through for the first time.

That was success. That was winning. It was just self-contained.

My goal.

My accomplishment.

My win.

If you're happy doing something you wanted to do, even if no one else knows you did, that's a win in my book. Go ahead and let yourself feel successful because, honestly, you are.

I set little goals and have little wins all the time. I do it with piano, but I do it with other things, too. I want to learn Spanish. Well, actually, I want to be multilingual, I'm just starting with Spanish. The first time I tried Rosetta Stone Spanish, I failed. It was so frustrating. No matter what I said or how I said it, the computer always said I was wrong. These days, I'm understanding more and pronouncing things better, so I'm finding some success. Every lesson with a green check mark is a win. And I'll just keep chipping away at it until I'm done.

I dream about going to Mexico or Colombia or Venezuela or pretty much any Spanish-speaking country. Once I've learned Spanish, I wouldn't be alone when I traveled. I wouldn't just hear people talking to each other; I'd actually be able to understand them and even join in. Imagine having a conversation with somebody you've never met before in a different country! Or reading the news in another country in that country's language! Or being able to really, really understand the menu so you can choose something good to eat! Those are goals of mine, and I'm going to get those big wins someday—right now I'm setting up lots of smaller wins along the way.

I do that a lot. I keep setting tiny goals and chipping away at things even when part of me wants to stop. It's because of a quote I heard one time: "Success is usually right around the corner." Every time I think of quitting, I think of that quote. I've seen the same thing as a meme on Instagram. There's a person hacking through this rock wall. Finally, they just give up. They're like, "I've had enough." But in the illustration, you see that if they had just hit the rock wall a few more times, they would've gotten to what they wanted.

I'm a firm believer in that philosophy. That's why I don't quit. When I get the urge to quit, I imagine how close I am to success, and then I push past it. I guess it's kind of like FOMO. I think how sad someone would be seeing the cartoon version of me just two inches from being fluent in Spanish, and that helps me find the energy to take another swing. Maybe I take a rest first, but I almost always take another swing. Because here's the cool thing about getting to decide what is success: you also get to decide when to quit. If you haven't quit, you haven't lost. You just haven't won yet.

Being a competitive speller is good practice for learning not to quit. Even for the best spellers, spelling is kind of an on-and-off thing. No one gets first place every time. The first time I entered a SpellPundit bee to practice for Scripps, I had recently gotten a spelling tutor, but I hadn't been working with my tutor long enough yet to see a big difference. I entered the spelling bee anyway. I eventually wanted to win Scripps, and I knew I needed more practice in spelling bees. I set a goal for myself: maybe I wouldn't win the SpellPundit bee, but no matter what, I wouldn't get below sixth place.

When the bee didn't go the way I wanted, I felt sorry for myself for a little while. I asked myself, "How did this happen? This is not me. This is not who I am." Then I imagined myself chipping away at that rock wall again, and I entered the next spelling bee.

A lot of people don't realize that I competed in the 2019 Scripps National Spelling Bee. Just being eligible to participate in 2019 means that I was already an elite speller. Everyone competing was an elite speller. Only one person can get first place. Actually, that's not true. In 2019, there were eight people in first place, something that had apparently never happened before. But I was not one of those eight, and if I were a person who chose people as my opponents, I would have had eight new enemies. I'm not going to sit here and say I didn't have a lot of feelings when I didn't make the final round in 2019. Mixed up in those feelings was happiness for the eight first-place spellers. I knew they must have worked hard, and I knew how devastating it would have been for them to hear the bell ring. I know it was for me.

After the Scripps National Spelling Bee in 2019, I had a moment where I was like, "I'm sick of this. Do I really wanna do this again?" I let myself think about that for a few minutes. It might have even been half an hour, but after that I had to kick that thought to the curb and get back to work. There was no way I was going to stop there. If I stopped there, I would have officially lost, and not because of missing first place. I would have lost because of quitting on my own goal. I would have lost in my own heart. As soon as I decided that wasn't where my story would end, that moment turned from a dead end into a stepping-stone. I could literally see myself chipping away at that rock wall, getting closer and closer to my goal.

I already had my family, a support system of people I loved and cared for who loved and cared for me right back. I wasn't afraid to be myself, a quirky, curious reader/scientist/athlete/big sister with an intense passion for spelling. I knew exactly what I was up against, and I had just asked for help and gotten even more of it in the form of Cole. It was up to me to roll with the punches so that I could meet my goal and win . . . my way.

It was rough, but I love spelling, and even though I wasn't 100 percent certain that I'd make it if I kept going, I was 100 percent certain that if I quit, I would never win. That was enough to help me push the negativity aside and chip away at the wall a few more times. So, instead of stopping there and trying to convince myself that I never liked spelling much anyway, I started working with Cole to get a new system in place. Cole's system helped me dig deep again. Yes, I was digging into root words, but I was also kind of digging deeper into myself. Every swing at that imaginary rock wall made me feel stronger and better because I was getting stronger and better. And I was proud of myself. I was proud of myself because I had been tested, and I knew for sure I wouldn't quit on myself. That felt good.

How does that Japanese proverb go? "Fall down seven times, stand up eight"? It doesn't matter how many times you fail. How many words you misspell. How many times your colors don't blend the right way or how many times your skateboard doesn't catch air. What matters is that you try again until you win. Once you win, all the rest will fade away.

I didn't win the Scripps National Spelling Bee in 2019, but that is not my story. I wouldn't let it be. I kept going. I got up and tried again, and guess what? So can you. That's not bragging. It's just true.

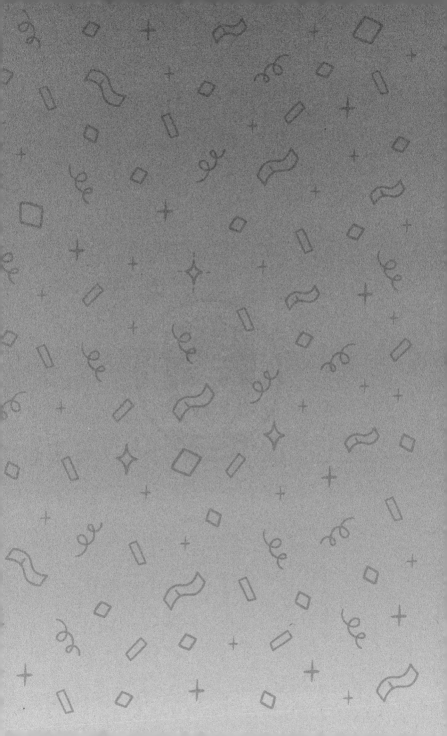

OUTRO

So, there you have it. Those are the nine things that help me level up my skills and, hopefully, grow in the process. I hope I didn't make it sound easy, because it's not easy. But I also hope I made it sound possible, because it is possible, especially if you remember that you are amazing and you're not alone. I need reminders about that, too. The whole "It's not bragging if it's true" thing isn't mine. It's a reminder that comes from my mom. I cringe pretty much every time she says it, but I have to admit that she's right. None of us can be our best selves if we're afraid of saying what we're good at. If you've worked to get good at something, sharing it isn't bragging, boasting, showing off, or tooting your own horn. There's a time and a place for everything, and that includes talking about what you're good at. I hope this book will help you want to grow your strengths and then share them with the whole world, or even just the people you trust the most. Someone will be there to encourage you on the path to becoming the ultimate *you*.

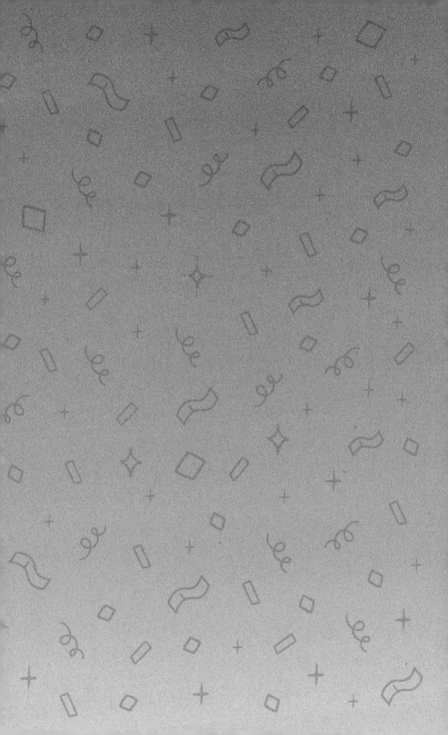

ACKNOWLEDGMENTS

Without all the people in my life who have encouraged me to reach greater heights, I honestly would not be here. I have an entire community of people behind me, enough to write an entire acknowledgment book, but I am not going to do that.

First and foremost, I would like to thank my parents, Alma Heard and Jawara Spacetime—first, for my existence, and second, for putting me in the position to do all the things I have done that have led to the writing of this book. I would like to thank my grandparents Jackie Knightshade and Irvin Heard for their endless support and for eating my air food when they would come to visit when I was little. I want to thank my spelling tutor, Cole Shafer-Ray, for tutoring me for about a year, and Snehaa Ganesh Kumar and her mother, Vijaya Nagharajhen, for providing me with valuable assistance in the final months of my spelling career. And finally, I would like to thank all the little girls out there for inspiring me as I wrote this book.

Oh yeah, I would also like to give a big thanks to my three little brothers, Sol, Zwe, and Wonder, for distracting me while I was studying. Seriously, you guys are the best!

TURN THE PAGE

FOR A *NEW*, EXCLUSIVE INTERVIEW WITH ZAILA.

KEEP READING TO FIND OUT WHAT SHE'S BEEN UP TO AND WHAT SHE'S PLANNING NEXT!

You won the Scripps National Spelling Bee in 2021 and took the country by storm. What have you been up to since then?

Since I won Scripps, I've mostly been focusing on my basketball career and, of course, school. I've also participated in some supercool programs like High School Aerospace Scholars (HAS) and Genes in Space.

You've made headlines for your basketball skills, setting multiple Guinness World Records and gaining recognition from NBA players, such as LeBron James and Stephen Curry. Can we look forward to any more record-setting feats soon?

You never know—I'm leaving my options open!

Congratulations on becoming a *New York Times* best-selling author with *It's Not Bragging If It's True*! How does it feel to achieve such success with your first book?

It's an amazing feeling! When I was a young girl reading my favorite books, if you had told me that one day I would be writing my own books, let alone a *New York Times* bestseller, let's just say that I wouldn't have believed you.

And how has the response been at home among your friends and family? Did your little brothers have anything to say about this latest accomplishment?

My whole extended family is super proud of me, which makes me feel very uplifted, and all my friends were also very proud of me. I think my little brothers are largely ambivalent to the whole affair! I'm still just their annoying older sister, I guess.

 Has life been any different for you since the book came out? Have you noticed any changes in your interactions with people in your community?

Since the book came out, I would say that the main thing that's changed is that I always need to make sure I have a Sharpie with me in case somebody wants their book signed.

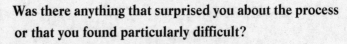 **Having now been a part of the whole publishing process, from turning an idea into a book all the way to seeing that book released into the world, what was your favorite part?**

My favorite part was definitely the press tour and getting to visit the Penguin Random House headquarters. It was awesome to finally get to meet all the people (and it was a lot of people) who contributed to making my dream of publishing a book come true.

Was there anything that surprised you about the process or that you found particularly difficult?

The only thing that surprised me a bit was just how detailed the process was. I already knew that it's a very painstaking process to make a book perfect, but to actually experience it up close was a bit startling.

What was your goal in writing *It's Not Bragging If It's True,* and what do you want readers to take away from the book?

My goal in writing *It's Not Bragging If It's True* was to provide my personal blueprint to how I became successful. Obviously, everybody is different, so not everything I did may benefit everybody, but my hope was that everybody would be able to take at least a little bit from what I wrote.

Some big changes have taken place since you wrote the book. You're now a couple of years older, and your whole family has relocated from Louisiana to Washington, DC. How has the adjustment been with everything you've had going on for the book as well?

It's been great! The process of moving was very smooth, and we all love where we live now. And of course, Washington, DC, is closer to New York City, which is where all the preparations for my book were, so . . . I guess it was a win-win.

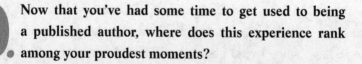

Now that you've had some time to get used to being a published author, where does this experience rank among your proudest moments?

I would say that this is tied for my second-proudest moment. Obviously, nothing will overtake my pride in winning Scripps, and having the Guinness World Record for most basketballs dribbled by one person is supercool, too.

11. And how about among your most difficult moments? Which is harder: dividing five-digit numbers by two-digit numbers in your head or writing a book?

Hmm . . . I'll definitely say that dividing five-digit numbers by two-digit numbers in my head is harder. But I do it easily. ;)

12. Breaking records, winning the Scripps National Spelling Bee, writing books—you've done it all! Given your long list of impressive achievements, what motivates you to keep going?

The main thing that keeps me going is just the desire to keep achieving. I really like finding new challenges and conquering them, which in turn gives me a high level of confidence for when I go on to the next challenge, kind of creating a positive feedback loop.

13. You have become a role model for so many people, and this book is a great example of why. Is there anyone you consider a role model?

I have a whole bunch of role models, but some of my main ones are Mae Jemison and Malala Yousafzai. Ever since I read about them when I was younger, I've been super inspired by their stories and their perseverance. Seeing how they overcame all kinds of obstacles made me realize that I can quite literally do anything.

14. **What is the biggest lesson you have learned over the last few years of having a book published and being in the public eye?**

The biggest thing I've learned since being in the spotlight is that "you never know who's watching." I genuinely believe that being in the public eye has made me a better person. I say this because when you know that there are a whole bunch of little boys and girls who look up to you, are watching you, and will be disappointed if you slip up, it makes you stay on your p's and q's.

15. **You've set records, both on the basketball court and the spelling bee stage, and you've inspired a nation. What comes next for you?**

I really don't know right now! This year, I'm actually no longer going to be homeschooled. That's right! I'm going to be attending high school, so that's going to be interesting. Mostly, I'm just working on my basketball career and preparing for my first year of school.

AND HERE ARE SOME

PHOTOS OF ME

THROUGHOUT THE YEARS!

Hanging out with my dad in Washington, DC. Wasn't I the cutest?

Posing for the camera in my favorite childhood park in New Orleans. I loved that hat so much.

Me and my little brother Sol with our baby brother, Zwe

I started playing basketball at age five—this photo was
taken even before then. Note the backward dress.

Me as a baller-ina in my living room/training room

$$\text{iii. } 137 - \frac{413496}{7550} =$$

$$\text{iv. } \frac{1034350}{7550} - \frac{413496}{7550} = \frac{620854}{7550}$$

$$\text{i. } 52\% \left(2\frac{1}{4}v - \frac{8}{5}\right) = \sqrt{144} + 5^2 - \frac{8}{10}v \qquad \text{Left 1520/1/}$$

$$\text{ii. } \frac{13}{25}\left(\frac{9}{4}v - \frac{8}{5}\right) = 12 + 125 - \frac{4}{5}v$$

$$\text{iii. } \frac{-4}{5}v - \frac{104}{125} = 137 - \frac{4}{5}v$$

$$\text{iv. } \frac{91}{25}v + \frac{4}{5}v = 137 + \frac{104}{125}$$

$$\text{v. } \frac{151}{25}v = \frac{17229}{125}$$

$$\text{vi. } \frac{151}{25} \cdot \frac{151}{25}v = \frac{17229}{125} \div \frac{151}{25}$$

$$\text{vii. } v = \frac{51687}{755}$$

Seven years old, smiling sheepishly next to my own mathematical handiwork

Hiding behind all six of my balls while getting ready for my Guinness World Records title attempt for dribbling basketballs simultaneously

Two of my favorite pastimes, snacking and reading :)

Getting ready for a game with the Nola Jazz, a New Orleans–based boys' travel team

Hanging out with my mom, back when I was shorter than she was

Practicing my unicycling skills. People are always surprised that I learned to ride a unicycle before a bicycle.

On an official visit to the University of Maryland, with my mother and my grandfather/math teacher/physics teacher

Cheesing with my mom at approximately 5:37 a.m. the day after winning Scripps. I'm not much of a morning person. . . .

At an LA Sparks game with Sue Bird (former Seattle Storm player and all-time great). She was the person who eventually told me I'd been named *Sports Illustrated* SportsKid of the Year!

With my friends Adam Lefkoe, Shaquille O'Neal, Candace Parker, and Dwyane Wade (plus my mom) during my first appearance on *NBA on TNT*

At the Smithsonian's *FUTURES* with Bill Nye (the Science Guy). He was nice enough to record a video saying hello to my brother Zwe!

YEARLING

Turning children into readers for more than fifty years.

**Classic and award-winning literature for every shelf.
How many have you checked out?**